LEROY COLLINS LEON COUNTY PUBLIC LIBRARY

3 1260 00821 9951

W9-BJN-431

Sheep

by Peter Brady

Bridgestone Books

an Imprint of Capstone Press

Bridgestone Books are published by Capstone Press
818 North Willow Street, Mankato, Minnesota 56001
Copyright © 1996 by Capstone Press
All rights reserved
Printed in the United States of America

Library of Congress Cataloging-in-Publication Data
Brady, Peter. 1944–
    Sheep/Peter Brady
    p. cm.
    Includes bibliographical references and index.
    Summary: Introduces the farm animal which is raised for its meat and for its wooly coat.
    Includes a brief explanation of how to make yarn.
    ISBN 1-56065-351-5
    1. Sheep--Juvenile literature. [1. Sheep.] I. Title.
SF375.2.B735 1996
636.3--dc20

                                                    95-54162
                                                       CIP
                                                        AC

Photo credits
Peter Ford: 10
William Muñoz: cover, 4-8, 12-20

William Muñoz is a freelance photographer. He has a B.A. from the University of Montana. He has taken photographs for many children's books. William and his wife live on a farm near St. Ignatius, Montana, where they raise cattle and horses.

J 636.3 Bra
00821 9951   NEB 3/20/97
Brady, Peter, 1944-

Sheep /

EBS

Table of Contents

Words in **boldface** type in the text are defined in the
Words to Know section in the back of this book.

What Is a Sheep?

A sheep is a farm animal. Sheep are raised for their meat and for their woolly coats. Male sheep are called rams, and female sheep are called ewes (yoos).

What Sheep Look Like

Sheep have broad shoulders, heavy bodies, and short legs. Their wool can be long and shaggy or short and curly. Sheep can be black, white, brown, gray, or spotted.

Where Sheep Live

Sheep live on farms and ranches. Sheep have **waterproof** coats so they can stay outside most of the time. Sometimes in very bad weather, they stay in a barn.

What Sheep Eat

Sheep eat mostly grass. Sometimes they are fed grain. Sheep have no top front teeth. They swallow grass right away and bring it up later to chew.

Different Kinds of Sheep

There are more than 800 **breeds** of sheep. Some of them are Angora, Nubian, Dorset, Southdown, and Hampshire. Different breeds are raised for their different wools.

Shearing

Sheep grow thick wool coats for the winter. In the spring, the wool is sheared. The wool is cut off all in one piece. Wool from one sheep is called fleece. The fleece can weigh from three pounds (1.35 kilograms) to 20 pounds (nine kilograms).

Bleating

When a lamb is born, one of the first things it hears is its mother's **bleat**. The lamb bleats back. The ewe and lamb will recognize each other's bleat for the rest of their lives.

Lambs

Ewes usually give birth to two lambs in the spring. Lambs are also called kids. Lambs are frisky and playful. They usually stick close to their mothers.

What Sheep Give Us

Sheep give us the wool to make rugs and clothes such as jackets, sweaters, and scarves. Their skin is made into leather for gloves. People also eat their meat which is called mutton.

Hands On: How to Spin Yarn

Before wool can be made into clothing, it must be made into yarn. To learn to spin yarn, you can use a ball of cotton from the inside of a new pill bottle.

Hold the ball of cotton between your thumb and index finger. With the other hand, pinch a little of the cotton and pull it slowly. Twist the cotton as you pull.

Your cotton yarn should be strong and smooth. If your yarn is lumpy, you need to pull it more. If your yarn breaks easily, you need to twist it more.

Words to Know

bleat—the cry of a sheep

breed— group of animals that come from the same ancestors

waterproof—able to keep water from getting through

Read More

Fowler, Allan. *Woolly Sheep and Hungry Goats.* Chicago: Children's Press, 1993.

Paladino, Catherine. *Spring Fleece: A Day of Sheep Shearing.* Boston: Little, Brown, 1990.

Patent, Dorothy Hinshaw. *The Sheep Book.* New York: Dodd, Mead, 1985.

Royston, Angela. *Lamb.* New York: Lodestar, 1992.

Index